PERFORMANCE MARKETING

A PRACTICAL GUIDE ON PERFORMANCE MARKETING FOR BEGINNERS

CHRISTOPHER HOLMES

Copyright © 2022 CHRISTOPHER HOLMES

All rights reserved

The characters and events portrayed in this book are fictitious. Any similarity to real persons, living or dead, is coincidental and not intended by the author.

No part of this book may be reproduced, or stored in a retrieval system, or transmitted in any form or by any means, electronic, mechanical, photocopying, recording, or otherwise, without express written permission of the publisher.

CONTENTS

Title Page
Copyright
CHAPTER ONE — 1
CHAPTER TWO — 6
CHAPTER THREE — 12
CHAPTER FOUR — 17
CHAPTER FIVE — 26

CHAPTER ONE

INTRODUCTION

We throw around the word "digital marketing" so frequently. Digital marketing comes in a variety of forms, and each type's outlets and capabilities are expanding daily.

Performance marketing is one underutilized digital marketing tactic. Advertisers only receive payment with performance marketing when particular events take place. When a viewer clicks through to their page or purchases anything, for instance.

In this book, performance marketing will be thoroughly examined, including its principles, benefits, and best channels for application.

Performance marketing is a results-based approach to digital marketing. Because payment is dependent upon how users engage with the content, it's perfect for businesses looking to reach their audience at scale.

Performance marketing is a type of digital marketing in which brands only pay marketing service providers when their business goals have been achieved or when particular actions, like a click, sale, or lead, have been taken. It is, therefore, a form of performance-based marketing.

Advertising for a company is designed and placed on any number of performance marketing channels, including social media, search engines, videos, embedded web content, and more, by connecting advertisers with publishers or agencies. Instead of paying upfront for an advertisement as is customary, these advertisers pay according to how well their advertisement performs as measured by the number of clicks, impressions, shares, or sales.

How to Use Performance Marketing

Advertisers place their ads on a specific channel (more information on the best performance marketing channels is provided below), and they are then paid according to how well the ad performs. Regarding performance marketing, there are several different payment options:

Cost Per Click(CPC)

Advertisers are compensated according to the frequency of clicks on their ads. This is an effective way to increase traffic to your website.

Cost Per Impression(CPM)

Impressions are views of your advertisement. With CPM, you pay for every thousand views; for instance, if 25,000 people saw your advertisement, you would be charged your base rate multiplied by 25.

Cost Per Sale (CPS)

With CPS, you only pay when an advertisement contributed to a sale being made. Additionally, affiliate marketing frequently employs this system.

Cost Per Lead (CPL)
When someone registers for something, such as an email newsletter or webinar, you pay, similar to the cost per sale. CPL produces leads that you can follow up with to increase sales.

Cost per acquisition (CPA)
Similar to CPL and CPS but with a broader application is the cost per acquisition. With this setup, advertisers only get paid when customers take a certain action.

Excellent Performance Marketing Channels

Agencies and advertisers employ performance marketing in five different ways to increase traffic:

Banner (display) advertisements

If you've been online recently, you've probably seen a lot of display ads. These advertisements are displayed on the side of your Facebook newsfeed as well as at the top and bottom of the news website you were just on. Even though display ads are gradually losing their appeal as a result of the growing use of ad blockers and a phenomenon known as banner blindness, many businesses are still having success with display ads that make use of interactive content, videos, and eye-catching graphic design.

Native Marketing

To promote sponsored content, native advertising

makes use of a website's or page's organic design. For instance, sponsored videos might show up under "Watch Next" on a YouTube page. You may have noticed native ads on Facebook Marketplace, for example, which are also common on e-commerce websites. Native advertising is successful because it enables your sponsored content to coexist naturally with other types of original content. Users frequently fail to distinguish between these different types of content, which enables you to market your company in a way that seems natural.

Content Marketing

Educating your audience is the main goal of content marketing. Additionally, it generates three times as many leads as outbound marketing while costing 62 per cent less, according to OmniVirt. With content marketing, you put your brand in context while also giving users useful information. For instance, a vitamin company might publish several educational blog posts about the advantages of probiotics, linking them to the probiotics they sell. Blog posts, case studies, e-books, and other forms of content marketing are available.

Social Media

Social media is a haven for performance marketers. Users can share your sponsored content naturally, expanding your reach far beyond the original post, and giving you the chance to reach users and direct them to your website. Although Facebook has the most services available to performance marketers, other websites like

LinkedIn, Instagram, and Twitter also provide a wealth of chances to connect with potential clients.

Internet marketing (SEM)

Search engine marketing (SEM)-optimized websites are crucial because the majority of online research is done using search engines. Cost-per-click (CPC) is the main focus of performance marketing, particularly for paid advertising. Many performance marketers use content marketing and SEO-optimized landing pages for organic SEM.

Utilizing performance marketing channels can enable you to scale your advertising efforts to satisfy your company's needs without going over budget, especially as the future of digital marketing becomes more promising every year.

Performance marketing is a smart and efficient way to widen your target market and increase your reach, all the while gathering insightful data. The advantages also extend beyond that. You'll discover that expanding your business is simpler than ever when you embrace the full functionality of performance marketing, including sponsored social media posts, and native and affiliate advertising.

CHAPTER TWO

PERFORMANCE MARKETING BENEFITS

Performance marketing is a sort of paid marketing and advertising that is performance-based and in which a company only pays after the desired action is taken. These activities, which have been pre-agreed upon by the company (merchants) and the marketing partners (publishers), may take a variety of forms, including clicks, the creation of leads, and most often, a sale. Through performance marketing platforms or tools, marketers may assess how well they performed the aforementioned steps.

Several strategies may be used to implement marketing performance. A business may work with publishers (such as Facebook, Google, or more specialized websites) to develop marketing ads or branded content, which are subsequently shown on their platforms. In influencer marketing, the influencers serve as the publishers and advertise a business by sharing it on their social media channels and promoting it via their content (vlogs, social media postings, etc.). The business then compensates the publishers that aired the advertisement on their platform or promoted the business via their content when the desired action has been achieved.

Performance marketing prospects should be well

informed of the advantages a campaign may provide for their business. The top four benefits that performance marketing provides companies are as follows:

Cost-effective
Comparatively speaking, display advertising is far more expensive than performance marketing. Companies that use performance marketing only have to pay when a certain action is completed, as opposed to making an upfront payment regardless of the outcomes. This is a lot more cost-effective and results-driven method, especially if you're a small firm with a tight budget.

Because companies are explicitly defining their objectives and negotiating an optimum fee for each activity that is done, performance marketing also enables better planning. If a business decides on a conversion rate of $0.50 and expects to convert 1,000 leads, it may plan to invest $500 in the campaign.

Simple performance monitoring
Measurement of the success and efficacy of your company's marketing plan is made simpler with the help of performance marketing. Affise and Any track are two examples of digital performance marketing platforms that may be used for this. Owners of businesses won't have to hazard a guess or estimate as to how many leads came from a certain project. When an effort achieves the expected outcomes, whether it be a prospective consumer signing up for the business's marketing emails or clicking on an advertisement, these results are immediately recorded by the performance marketing tool of the business.

Additionally, these technologies will evaluate the raw data from marketing campaigns to offer the business a precise picture of its ROI. This gives businesses the ability to assess the effectiveness of both individual projects and bigger campaigns more effectively.

Objectivity
Business owners can estimate the return on their investment thanks to performance marketing. Platforms for marketing software provide performance monitoring and real-time outcomes so organizations can observe how intended activities are being accomplished in real-time. Additionally, they provide information on which partners are doing well in terms of clicks, subscribers, conversions, or other metrics, allowing companies to utilize this information to enhance their campaigns and increase their bottom line.

Risk-Free
Performance marketing involves less risk than other kinds of marketing efforts. The first benefit is that you only pay for requested activities after they have been completed, ensuring that you get what you paid for. Additionally, these campaigns are far more adaptable. Should their business have financial difficulties, business owners have the authority to make adjustments to their budget. If intended results are not being achieved, or if they are and the firm has spent all of its available funds, it may also halt campaigns completely.

How to Begin with Performance Marketing

Here are three actions you should do to get started with performance marketing if you believe your company is ready to utilize it to boost profits:

1. Define Your Objectives

Defining your company's objectives is the first stage in performance marketing. Are you in need of increasing website traffic? more lead generation? or turn leads into paying clients? Your decision about the metrics you'll use to gauge how successfully your objectives are being achieved will be influenced by the goals you've established. The platform(s) you'll employ to carry out your performance marketing campaign will also be determined by this.

2. Select the format for your advertising and search for opportunities.

The next stage is to decide how you want to market after you've determined your objectives. Here are some alternatives to think about:

Influencer advertising

This is sometimes accomplished by using micro-influencers—people with between 2,000 and 50,000 social media followers who, in certain situations, are authorities in a particular sector or speciality. You may try to collaborate with more well-known influencers who have greater followings depending on your company's budget, but this will be more costly. Because influencers will promote your business via their unique material while identifying it as an "ad," in return for a pre-agreed price, influencer marketing is more organic than traditional advertising.

Affiliate promotion

You may hire affiliate marketers to advertise and sell your brand to other people. After that, you would give them a commission for each sale they made.

Your business may work with publishers like Facebook and Google to develop branded content or advertisements that will run on their platforms. You should research to find publications that are relevant to your target market; this may also include specialized blogs and websites.

societal media Since the bulk of people spend their online time on social networking sites like Twitter, Instagram, LinkedIn, and similar ones, these are also fantastic venues to promote your company. Businesses should have their social media accounts on each of these sites where they may regularly promote their news, content, goods, etc. The benefit of this situation is that you can be sure your audience of followers is interested in your business because they follow you if they weren't.

3. Remember to monitor and evaluate your progress.

Last but not least, if you don't monitor or evaluate your performance, you won't know if your efforts have been effective or not. Use performance marketing software to get data and statistics that are essential for assessing the effectiveness of your campaign. This will enable you to assess your progress and identify your strongest areas so that you may concentrate more on them.

A company owner or marketer may still learn a lot from performance marketing. Some of the above-listed issues just scratch the surface. Performance marketing may, however, be a very useful tool for many small firms if used properly.

CHAPTER THREE

PERFORMANCE MARKETING CHALLENGES AND HOW TO OVERCOME THEM

Marketers must prepare for challenging times.

A recession is coming for the whole world's economy. This will probably result in prospective clients having lesser buying power. More than ever, marketers will need to provide evidence of their budgetary choices' effectiveness.

Performance marketing has evolved at the same time, as we can see. In the past, practically everything that ensured success in digital marketing was driven by third-party data, but this has changed.

Even Meta themselves have acknowledged that iOS14 has significantly decreased the accuracy of aiming and measuring.

1) Effective community and brand development
It used to be feasible to create an arbitrage-based business model. You might open an internet store, sell generic goods, purchase relevant traffic, and optimize it such that the cost of acquiring that traffic was less than the lifetime value of the clients you attracted. From here, you may grow your company and create a reliable brand-free entity.

Precise (almost spooky) targeting and reliable conversion attribution laid the framework for this completely. That's no longer the case thanks to the release of iOS14. This poses difficulties. The emergence of Shopify coincided with a steady rise in the number of stores selling a variety of goods. Today, there are hundreds of stores selling a wide variety of goods.

E-commerce enterprises thus need to understand how to set themselves out more than before. Building a powerful brand is the ideal (and often the only) method to do it. A brand that is ideally driven by individuals that are at the forefront. It's always been like that. But with the collapse of precise performance marketing, the need for creative brand creation in the media mix must rise once again. Only after this foundation is established can it be expanded upon and scaled up with advertising.

2) Tracking on the server
If your measurement infrastructure in this area is still using frontend javascript snippets, you should think about switching. Stable web & revenue monitoring is the cornerstone for successfully executing performance-based advertisements. Nearly all client-side tags no longer activate automatically on the internet today. You could only be monitoring a small portion of the information accessible.

The development of Universal Analytics will eventually come to an end, according to a recent announcement from Google Analytics. It will put all of its future efforts into GA4. Therefore, it will be worthwhile to put some money into putting up GTM Server-side & GA4 as your new measurement stack.

3) Internal data knowledge

Adverity has outlined the three pillars that high-performing marketing teams must adhere to become fully data-driven:

A firm can only become fully data-driven with the help of the appropriate culture, the right people, and the right technology.

Large volumes of data are available to businesses nowadays, and it takes a full-time job to make sense of it, transform it into insights, and draw actionable conclusions from it. It should not be outsourced since it calls for specialized talents and is so essential to the success of your company. A good data or business intelligence department may make all the difference, especially in these unpredictable times.

4) Pay attention to CRM and retention

The demise of third-party cookies will result in less precise advertising. This logically implies that the expense of gaining new clients is increasing. If you still want to be
profitable, you will need to find other sources of income than bringing in new clients.

Reactivating previous customers is a smart move in this case. The most cost-effective way to increase your customers' lifetime value and retention rate will be to market to them more often.

5) Modeling of market mix

Making informed budgeting choices depends on effectively calculating ROI for each of your marketing platforms. Therefore, your media purchase will certainly become less effective if you are unable to link income to marketing touchpoints. This is further supported by a recent BCG poll, which found that marketers anticipate a 22% decline in marketing ROI as a result of the impending depreciation of third-party cookies.

While marketers are looking for new technology that can still provide these insights, there is an unsung hero technology that is growing (again). Currently, the industry pays a lot of attention to market mix modelling.

Over 50 years have passed since the invention of the marketing mix modelling (MMM) tool. Most businesses in the RMG sector are probably already using it in some form. MMM uses statistical modelling to provide a top-down (aggregate) view of how advertising is performing for both active customers and acquisition, whereas attribution builds a picture of performance from the bottom up (user-level).

Despite being an outdated technology, many industry participants believe the time is right to predict a renaissance for it.

Why one may wonder?

Painting a complete data picture has always been the most difficult MMM task. The quality of the underlying dataset determines how well the model measuring the marketing mix performs. It was frequently both a technical and an organizational challenge for many companies to compile this gapless set of all marketing activities that took place over a specific period. However, the tools available today are the best for developing this single source of truth using all of your marketing data. You will be able to create a complete data picture by utilizing a powerful ETL tool along with in-house data expertise. And a good modelling technology applied to this data set has the potential to produce insights that are superior to what attribution modelling has ever been able to produce.

As a performance-driven marketing department, you will need to adapt due to numerous environmental changes.

While other new skills have emerged, some previously significant skills may have diminished in significance.

CHAPTER FOUR

PERFORMANCE MARKETING METRICS

To reach millions of potential customers who spend time online, businesses use digital marketing strategies. Marketing experts examine digital marketing metrics to gain knowledge of consumer behaviour and the cost of luring customers to company websites or social media platforms to assess the success of their campaigns and develop new strategies. Understanding these metrics will enable you to maximize your marketing initiatives and advance your company.

In this book, we outline the goals and functions of digital marketing metrics and provide a list of 15 significant metrics that are frequently employed in the sector.

What do metrics in digital marketing mean?

The success of a company's online marketing initiatives is gauged by using digital marketing metrics, also known as key performance indicators (KPIs). To monitor and analyze how customers engage with your brand on websites and social media platforms, digital marketing metrics are used.

With the help of targeted campaigns or more general marketing initiatives, businesses can analyze the strategies they used to reach both existing and potential customers by using digital marketing metrics. Additionally, by using these metrics, marketers can discover fresh ways to tailor their strategies for boosting customer acquisition and brand recognition. Digital marketing metrics can also direct professionals away from potentially ineffective campaign strategies so they can focus their efforts more effectively on successful ones.

Digital marketing metrics display a variety of information that may have an impact on spending, advertising, and sales forecasts. These metrics are determined by marketing professionals using software programs that calculate specific numbers or website analysis tools from online vendors.

Here are the top digital marketing metrics that experts in the field use to gauge the success and profitability of their initiatives:

1. Search engine optimization (SEO) and key phrases
To increase website traffic and evaluate results, marketing professionals use search engine optimization as both a strategy and a metric. Using keywords, SEO creates natural search results that can increase the number of visitors to your website. The main keywords that are pertinent to your website are analyzed using SEO metrics, and it is possible to see how keyword strategies have increased traffic to your website's content by looking at how many people have visited it.

2. Total traffic to the website

Measuring the overall volume of visitors to your website can help you get a better overall understanding of where your traffic is coming from, how many potential customers are stopping by, and any trends in the number of visitors over time. Businesses strive to generate consistent increases in the volume of traffic to their websites.

You can get a general idea of your online presence by looking at the number of visitors to your website. The effectiveness of a campaign to attract visitors to your website, which may then convert into customer purchases, can be determined by looking at your total website traffic.

Channel Traffic

You can assess which strategies are the most efficient for attracting visitors by looking at how visitors got to your site. Marketing experts investigate where online users went before visiting their website and how users got there by using the channel traffic metric. This includes the subsequent channel options:

Direct traffic

Users who directly visit your website do so by typing its URL into the browser's top search bar. With no assistance from a search engine or other channel, this directs customers to your website. Direct traffic from visitors with high intent reveals great brand awareness. Organic search results are the links that show up in between sponsored advertisements when users enter a particular phrase into a search engine. This is a component of SEO that makes use of keywords to increase the likelihood of top search engine results.

Social media platforms:
Consumers may access your website from another channel by clicking on links posted there. Posts from your accounts and clicking on social media-based advertisements are two examples of this.

3. Referrals
Visitors to your website could discover it via a link or reference on another website. This could be done via guest blogging, collaborations with influencers, or joint ventures with other companies.

4. Inversions
Marketers may see how many website visits are converted to subscribers or paying customers using conversion statistics. Users who download material from your website are also included in conversion analytics. Increased website traffic is intended to convert users into customers since this results in more direct sales or followers. Higher conversion rates are a sign of good marketing initiatives, appealing site content, and persuasive product incentives.

5. Standard bounce rate
Bounce rates reveal the number of visitors that abandoned your website after just seeing one page. You can find out, the second, how long visitors stayed on your website before departing thanks to bounce rate stats. The bounce rate increases in significance as the

duration decreases. Low bounce rates show that visitors are satisfied with the material they discover and are prepared to spend some time on your website, which may result in more potential conversions rather than lost possibilities.

6. Search engine trends

The way people access your website from organic search results is studied by search trends. Keyword trends may indicate that blog posts and landing pages need to be updated. Depending on your sector, trends could change according to known patterns, such as seasonal surges in organic traffic for certain goods or services. To evaluate annual variations in search results and identify high and low traffic times, you may also utilize search trends from specific data periods.

7. First-time visitors

Marketing experts may gauge the effectiveness of focused initiatives like banner adverts and strategic alliances by tracking the number of new visits to a site. Examining new visitors on a daily, weekly, or monthly basis, may also be used to evaluate the efficacy of fresh material. The proportion of new visitors to overall traffic is often provided by website analytic software.

8. Repeat visitors

Assessing the frequency of repeat visits may also reveal how valuable the information on your website is. Return visits are an indication of interest and timely information that is both appealing to your audience and timeless.

9. Information about the population's demographics

To learn more about the characteristics of their website users, marketers employ demographic data. Their decisions about where to position advertisements and how to provide the finest content for their target market are aided by this information.

10. Brand consciousness

A brand's success in the overall market may be inferred from anecdotal evidence such as brand mentions in third-party reviews and social media discussions, even if brand awareness can be a difficult statistic to quantify with precise numerical data. The following techniques may be used to assess brand awareness:

Consumers that do brand searches on search engine websites do so by typing in your brand name. This is a different metric for assessing organic traffic.

11. Likes on social media posts

Counting likes on social media posts enables you to determine how many people are interacting with or using your website.

Shares of your social media material by users are another indicator of the level of online brand awareness that has been created. Reposting material from your company's page is one option here.

Social media comments

Comments reveal that customers are interacting with your brand, which is a sign of its popularity online.

Number of followers

A clear sign of brand recognition is the number of people who follow your brand on social media websites. Gaining more followers can boost website traffic and show that your marketing efforts were successful.

Online conversations or brand mentions are examples of brand awareness. To assist identify how to reshape a brand's online reputation, marketing experts monitor both good and negative remarks.

12. Click-through rate

The proportion of individuals who choose to visit your website after clicking on an advertisement is measured by click-through rates. The majority of customers may notice your advertisement, but only a tiny percentage will click on it, according to marketing experts. Professionals aim for high views or impressions so that more people will click on the ads. Professionals in marketing should strive to increase click-through rates since it may result in more leads.

Response rate

Response rates for digital marketing messages demonstrate the number of people who respond or research firm offerings. This might refer to the number of subscribers who respond to a survey issued by email newsletter or if prospective customers fill out a business interest form. Marketing experts can determine the number of leads created by marketing initiatives by analyzing response rates. Increasing response rates also aids marketing teams in making more informed financial decisions to maximize return on investment (ROI).

13. Cost per click and cost per impression

Businesses pay for the right to have their advertisements appear on certain websites as part of digital marketing initiatives. Marketing experts may evaluate a cost per click or impression to assess the effectiveness of their advertising campaigns. In digital marketing circumstances, an impression denotes a person's online viewing of an advertisement, but a click denotes the user visiting your website after selecting to click on the advertisement.

Impressions are often estimated in big numbers, such as 1,000 impressions for a particular amount, as they don't always result in action and are less expensive than clicks. Because they are more likely to result in leads or even customers, businesses pay a greater cost per click.

14. Price per lead

A business's cost per lead is determined by elements such as impressions, clicks, and response rates. This indicator shows the entire cost of turning site visitors into prospective buyers, whether via advertising campaigns or organic traffic. Marketing experts may assess the financial success of their advertising campaigns by understanding their cost per lead. It may help with planning the budget and allocating money for certain initiatives. The cost per lead also enables marketers to determine the appropriate lead volume for the business.

15. Pageviews

You may examine the number of pages a person has visited in addition to how much time they spent on your website. The most popular section of your website may also be shown via pageviews. Online shopping pages may be the most popular on websites that support e-commerce, whilst informative blogs may be the most popular area of websites for service providers. You may strategically position content on these pages by knowing where people browse your website the most.

CHAPTER FIVE

STARTING YOUR FIRST CAMPAIGN

If you want to lower your acquisition expenses while raising your ROI, you could find yourself considering a performance marketing approach.

Fortunately, performance marketing initiatives aren't extremely difficult to start up and aren't overly complex.

This is a relatively new marketing strategy overall, made popular by the growing popularity of the platforms that make it possible. However, it is a strategy that will endure.

.Marketers and businesses alike like a strategy that can be evaluated, quantified, and won. Performance marketing provides the tools to achieve both thanks to the all-revealing measurements and analytics accessible as well as the distinct, palpable results that it consistently generates.

The primary result? Everyone is pleased as a consequence of more conversions, better outcomes, enhanced ROI, and less money squandered. Certain formats are more attractive than others and not all businesses should use them.

Steps to Planning a Performance Marketing Campaign

Establish a clear objective that supports your company.

Your whole digital marketing plan or growth strategy should be closely related to this. What do you intend to gauge? What objectives exist? Do you want to grow your email list? Do you intend to offer any products? You could wish to increase the number of individuals who read your eBook each month by a factor of 10.

Define it, comprehend how to quantify it, and then everyone will be in agreement moving forward. By being laser-focused on the objective at hand, the marketer will be able to maximize return on investment thanks to this feeling of clarity.

Select logical marketing channels.
Not every component of the jigsaw fits together, and not every marketing strategy will be the best choice for your company. You shouldn't assume something will work for you just because it did for someone else. Every component of marketing involves some degree of trial and error, but you can minimize this by taking the time to understand your customers and their habits (be sure your purchasing personas are perfect). You can make sure you're promoting correctly and at the appropriate location by knowing who they are and where they hang out.

Create your material in preparation for the campaign launch.
You'll immediately consider the kind of material you'll be posting while you're thinking about those channels. There are several content possibilities available,

including an in-depth, lengthy piece of material on your blog, images and captions on Instagram, and explainer videos. Understanding your audience is essential once again.

Keep an eye on and improve your campaign.
Never will a marketing effort be created and then forgotten. That is not who they are. You almost surely will be leaving money on the table if you start a campaign and then give it no attention later. Performance marketing is completely reliant on data and analytics. Almost always, there is an opportunity for development. Examine what is working and think about growing it; identify what is not and repeat or abandon it. It only makes sense to seek ways to further utilize it if you identify the top sources of leads or revenue.

Review and adjust as necessary
It's important to take stock after a campaign is over. Examine what worked and what didn't, then prepare to change it the next time. People often do this after failing campaigns to figure out what went wrong, but successful efforts may also benefit from this method.

Effective Channels For Performance Marketing Campaigns

When it comes to performance marketing, there's no need to invent the wheel. After all, hundreds of businesses have found success with similar efforts.

Finding the appropriate channel and strategy for your particular firm is the true challenge.

Channels for Performance Marketing on Social Media

Social media marketing is undoubtedly one of the most well-known performance marketing strategies available today, helped by some of the largest personalities in the public arena. Many marketers will provide social media marketing, but the primary challenge is that social media campaigns are simple to execute but challenging to make them yield results.

When starting a campaign like this, your goals should be to drive traffic to your website or pages, raise brand recognition, and ultimately convert those visitors into leads, sales, and customers. Typically, you'll track CPC, CPS, CPL, and more channel-specific behaviours like Likes on Facebook or Followers on Twitter (Twitter).

Facebook advertisements typically cost £1.72 for each click. You'll also come across measures like CPx, which charges you based on how many times someone views or interacts with your advertisement. For this statistic, Facebook is often more costly than Instagram.

Enabling platforms for social media marketing

- Facebook\sLinkedIn\sTwitter\sInstagram
- Reddit
- Pinterest
- Dispatch Marketing

Display advertising is often what the ordinary member of the public envisions when they think of internet advertising. After all, display advertising explains the popularity of tools like AdBlockers. These are the picture, audio, and video advertisements that may be seen on websites all over the internet. They can be rich media, sidebars, or banners.

Display advertising isn't often thought of in the same context as performance marketing. The normal clickthrough rate and actions are done in response to display advertising are, as you would expect, rather low. Rather than aiming for actions or conversions, many utilize it to promote brand recognition. But rather than taking a general strategy, the astute marketer would search for specialized and targeted display marketing chances. For the greatest results, identify the websites that your clients frequent and target them with display advertising there.

If you were to utilize Google's platform, you may anticipate paying an average of up to $0.58 per click.

Enabling platforms for display advertising

- Celtra\sAdroll\sChoozle
- A platform for Google Marketing
- Internet Advertising (SEM)
- SEM, which should not be confused with SEO, is one of the most widely employed kinds of digital marketing today, and for good reason. Results from search engine marketing initiatives will be seen by

the typical user many times each day.

Search engine marketing tools are available from Google, Bing, and Yahoo, and they all make campaign setup straightforward. Effective targeting and regular account audits may provide amazing outcomes. You may find the advertising at the top of the SERP by using one of the search engines to look for a service, item, or location.

The bulk of campaigns will be CPC-focused, meaning that you will be paid each time an ad is clicked. In actuality, you practically never pay anything until someone clicks an advertisement. However, SEM has advanced greatly in recent years, and you can now base campaigns on metrics like ROAS (Return on Ad Spend), conversions (based on trackers on your website), and more.

It depends on what the person discovers when they arrive at your website and isn't always accurate to focus just on CPC, but generally, you'll pay $2.32 per click with a cost per action of around $59.18. Consequently, your conversion rate will probably be about 3.9% on average.

SEM-facilitating platforms:

- Ads by Google
- Bing
- Yahoo
- Affiliate Promotion

Although there are platforms or marketplaces for affiliate marketing that link individuals together, the majority of affiliate marketing is done via direct relationships between marketers and companies. Marketer uses their connections and network to move leads and sales in the direction of your company. Then, often on a predetermined percentage basis, they will take a portion of the sales they refer to you. Many affiliates will hunt for programs that, in response to their performance, raise that proportion.

Typically seen on blog platforms, YouTube, live streaming, and other social media sites are sponsored content. These are the pieces of content that are published on well-known channels by individuals with sizable followings and are supported by a firm or business. Usually, they'll spread the word about the product or service they want to market, ask that people routinely mention it, sell it, and then expect that sales will result from positive word of mouth.

The vast majority of well-known YouTubers will advertise sponsored material, and other platforms will likely follow their example. In many nations, it is currently required by law for broadcasters to disclose whether a piece of entertainment contains commercial promotion. Likewise with affiliate marketing.

Sponsored material varies greatly in price. The size of the audience and the channel's popularity are often to blame for this. To have a piece of content sponsored, many of the bigger networks will have certain procedures and ways to follow. Even if they make it up on a case-by-case basis, smaller suppliers often reply to direct queries and provide pricing lists.

The most crucial idea to remember is that performance marketing only works if you are completely transparent from the start. If you are upfront about what you anticipate happening, reaching your objectives will be simple.

Make your objectives very clear.

Choose the best channel for your company.
After the campaign launches, monitor it and make any corrections and adjustments,
Introspection and campaign evaluation, whether effective or not
The final stage is to start the campaign, monitor the results, and take pleasure in the rewards of your hard work once you've thought through your objectives, planned the channels, and organized your campaign.

FAQs on Performance Marketing

Q1.What is performance-based marketing,
A digital marketing strategy driven by outcomes is called performance-based marketing. Payments are made to marketing service providers only after the business objectives, such as a click, sale, or lead, have been achieved, making it appropriate for brands that want to reach their audience at scale.

Q2. Is performance-based marketing fraudulent?
It is not a scam and performance marketing is legitimate. For businesses, it is a very valuable sector. You might be charged fees based on performance, and the advertiser might only use that money for brand

bidding and remarketing.

Q3. Why is performance-based marketing advantageous?

You can scale your advertising efforts and adhere to the needs of the business cost-effectively by using performance marketing channels. It is a successful strategy for broadening your audience. By implementing a trackable and manageable plan, you can widen your audience and collect insightful data.

Q4

How does performance marketing fit into the picture?

Performance marketing is a key component of online marketing strategies that help businesses attract new customers and keep existing ones. It causes measurable user responses or business transactions, enabling businesses to grow.

Q5. Should I put in place a performance marketing strategy?

Implementing a performance marketing plan can speed up your ability to connect with your target market if you are just starting in business. Through affiliates, it will assist you in increasing website traffic and brand awareness. Performance marketing is also accountable and measurable. Every buyer's entire click-to-consume path is visible, allowing you to determine which channels lead to the best outcomes. The absence of prepayment is crucial. As a result, the risk is lower.

Q6: What distinguishes digital marketing from performance marketing?

With performance marketing, you only pay when a specific outcome materializes in digital marketing. The term "digital marketing" is inclusive of a wide range of tactics, financing schemes, and distribution channels.

Q7: Should I hire outside help or can I handle performance marketing on my own?

Any business can independently engage in performance marketing if it has the resources (in-house marketing team size, budget, expertise, and bandwidth) to do so. In that case, it would be best to use reliable outside sources.

Q8: What distinguishes brand marketing from performance marketing?

Performance marketing is a form of advertising in which clients of marketing firms are compensated only after the completion of a given action, such as the generation of leads or sales. In contrast, brand marketing focuses on strategies that involve consumers and work to enhance positive consumer perceptions of the brand.

www.ingramcontent.com/pod-product-compliance
Lightning Source LLC
Chambersburg PA
CBHW050322220526
45465CB00005B/2092